The Star & the Garter

By
Aleister Crowley

Copyright © 2020 Lamp of Trismegistus. All rights reserved. No part of this publication may be reproduced or transmitted in any form or by any means, electronic or mechanical, including photocopying, recording, or by any information storage and retrieval system, without permission in writing from Lamp of Trismegistus. Reviewers may quote brief passages.

ISBN: 978-1-63118-406-2

Esoteric Classics

Other Books in this Series and Related Titles

The Poem of Hashish by A Crowley & C Baudelaire (978-1-63118-484-0)

Thirty-One Hymns to the Star Goddess by Frater Achad (978-1-63118-422-2)

A Collection of Magical Writings, Fiction, Poetry & Essays
By Aleister Crowley (978-63118-424-6)

Crystal Vision Through Crystal Gazing by Achad (978-1-63118-455-0)

The Machinery of the Mind by Dion Fortune (978-1-63118-451-2)

The Hymns of Hermes by G. R. S. Mead (978-1-63118-405-5)

Magical Essays and Instructions by Florence Farr (978-1-63118-418-5)

Rosa Alchemica, The Tables of Law & The Adoration of the Magi
by William Butler Yeats (978-1-63118-421-5)

Gnosis of the Mind by G. R. S. Mead (978-1-63118-408-6)

A Collection of Fiction and Essays by Occult Writers on Supernatural, Metaphysical and Esoteric Subjects by various (978-1-63118-712-4)

Qabbalistic Teachings and the Tree of Life by M P Hall (978-1-63118-482-6)

Rosicrucian Rules, Secret Signs, Codes and Symbols by various (978-1-63118-488-8)

The Sepher Yetzirah and the Qabalah by M P Hall (978-1-63118-481-9)

The Janeites, The Man Who Would Be King and Other Stories of Freemasonry
by Rudyard Kipling (978-1-63118-480-2)

The Path of Light: A Manual of Maha-Yana Buddhism (978-1-63118-471-0)

The Mysteries of Freemasonry & the Druids by M P Hall &c (978-1-63118-444-4)

Confessions of an English Opium-Eater by T De Quincey (978-1-63118-485-7)

Arcane Formulas or Mental Alchemy by W W Atkinson (978-1-63118-459-8)

The Leadbeater Reader: A Selection of Occult Essays (978-1-63118-483-3)

Audio versions are also available on Audible, Amazon and Apple

Table of Contents

Introduction...6

The Star & the Garter...9

INTRODUCTION

The word "esoteric" can be difficult to define. Esotericism in general can be seen less as a system of beliefs and more as a category, which encompasses numerous, different systems of beliefs. It's a bit of juxtaposition, since the word "esoteric" indicates something that few people know about, while the term itself broadly covers numerous philosophies, practices, areas of study and belief systems.

In a greater sense, Esotericism acts as a storehouse for secret knowledge, which is often considered ancient (by *tradition, if not by fact),* passed down from generation to generation, in private. At various times in history, simply possessing the knowledge of some of these subjects, was considered illegal and a jailable offence, if discovered. This usually included such general topics as Alchemy, Pharmacology, Qabalah, Hermeticism, Occultism, Ceremonial Magic, Astrology, Divination, Rosicrucianism and so on. Collectively, these areas of study were often referred to as the esoteric sciences.

Sometimes, the outer garment of a subject isn't esoteric, while what is hidden beneath it, is. As an example, Freemasonry isn't necessarily esoteric by nature (at *least not anymore),* but certain signs, passwords and handshakes given to the candidate during their initiation, are in fact, esoteric, in the sense that they are hidden from the general public.

Today, in the twenty-first century, such topics are readily available at bookstores across the country, and numerous mainsteam publishers offer beginners guides and coffee-table volumes on many of these subjects, intended for mass appeal. Books like *"The Secret"* have turned previously arcane topics into household knowledge. All that being the case, however, it isn't to say that there still aren't buried secrets to uncover, ancient wisdom being ignored and forgotten mysteries to be explored. In fact, it is often that we are only able to further our own studies by standing on the shoulders of these disappearing giants.

Lamp of Trismegistus is doing its part to help preserve humanity's esoteric history by making some of these classics available to those students who are seeking to unearth the knowledge of these ancient colossi.

So, be sure to check other titles from our *Esoteric Classics* series, as well as our *Occult Fiction, Theosophical Classics, Foundations of Freemasonry Series, Supernatural Fiction, Paranormal Research Series, Studies in Buddhism* and our *Christian Apocrypha Series.* You can also download the audio versions of most of these titles from Amazon, Apple or Audible, for learning on the go.

ΑΓΝΩΣΤΩ

ΘΕΩ

THE STAR AND THE GARTER

I

WHAT sadness closes in between
Your eyes and mine to-day, my Queen ?
In dewfall of our glance hath come
A chill like sunset's in hot lands
'Mid iris and chrysanthemum.
Well do I know the shaken sands
Within the surf, the beaten bar
Of coral, the white nenuphar
Of moonrise stealing o'er the bay.
So here's the darkness, and the day
Sinks, and a chill clusters, and I
Wrap close the cloak : then is it so
To-day, you rose-gleam on the snow,
My own true lover ? Ardently
I dare not look : I never looked
So : that you know. But insight keen
We (laugh and) call not " love." Now crooked
The light swerves somehow. Do you mean—
What ? There is coldness and regret
Set like the stinging winter spray
Blown blind back from a waterfall
On Cumbrian moors at Christmas. Wet
The cold cheek numbs itself. A way
Is here to make—an end of all ?
What sadness closes in between
Your eyes and mine to-day, my Queen ?

II

YOU are silent. That we always were.
The racing lustres of your hair
Spelt out its sunny message, though
The room was dusk : a rosy glow
Shed from an antique lamp to fall
On the deep crimson of the wall,
And over all the ancient grace
Of shawls, and ivory, and gems
To cast its glamour, till your face
The eye might fall upon and rest,
The temperate flower, the tropic stems.
You were silent, and I too. Caressed
The secret flames that curled around
Our subtle intercourse. Profound,
Unmoved, delighting utterly,
So sat, so sit, my love and I.
But not to-day. Your silence stirs
No answering rapture : you are proud,
And love itself checks and deters
The thought to say itself aloud.
Oh ! heart of amber and fine gold
Silverly darting lunar rays !
Oh ! river of sweet passion rolled
Adown invisible waterways !
Speak ! Did I wound you then unguessed ?
What is the sorrow unexpressed
That shadows those ecstatic lids ?
A word in season subtly rids
The heart of thoughts unseasonable.
You are silent. Do they speak in hell ?

III

IS it your glance that told me ? Nay !
I know you would not look that way.
Seeing, you strove to see not. Fool !
I have ruined all in one rash deed.
Learnt I not in discretion's school
The little care that lovers need ?
For see—I bite my lip to blood ;
A stifled word of anguish hisses :—
O the black word that dams thought's flood !
O the bad lip that looked for kisses !
O the poor fool that prates of love !
Is it a garter, or a glove ?

IV

A FOOL indeed ! For why complain,
Now the last five-barred gate is ope,
Held by a little boy ? I hope
The hour is handy to explain
The final secret. Have I any ?
Yes ! the small boy shall have a penny !
Now you are angry ? Be content !
Not fee the assistant accident
That shows our quarry—love—at bay ?
My silver-throated queen, away !
Huntress of heaven, by my side,
As moon by meteor, rushing, ride !
Among the stars, ride on ! ride on !
(Then, maybe, bid the boy begone !)

V

I AM a boy in this. Alas!
Look round on all the world of men!
The boys are oft of genus " ass."
Think yourself lucky, lady, then,
If I at least am boy. You laugh?
Not you! Is this love's epitaph,
God's worm erect on Herod's throne?
" Ah, if I only had not known ! "
All wrong, beloved! Truth be ours,
The one white flower (of all the flowers)
You ever cared for! Ignorance
May set its puppets up to dance;
We know who pulls the strings. No sage;
A man unwashed, the bearded brute!
His wife, the mother-prostitute!
Behind the marionetted stage
See the true Punch-and-Judy show,
Turn copper so to silver! Know,
And who can help forgiving? So
Said some French thinker. Here's a drench
Of verse unquestionably French
To follow! so, while youth is youth,
And time is time, and I am I,
Too busy with my work to lie,
Or love lie's prize—or work's, forsooth !—
Too strong to care which way may go
The ensuing history of woe,
Though I were jaw, and you were tooth;
So, more concerned with seeking sense

Than worried over consequence,
I'll speak, and you shall hear, the truth.

VI

TRUTH, like old Gaul, is split in three.
A lesson in anatomy,
A sketch of sociology,
A tale of love to end. But see !
What stirs the electric flame of eyes ?
One word—that word. Be destiny's
Inviolate fiat rolled athwart
The clouds and cobwebs of our speech,
And image, integrate of thought,
This ebony anthem, each to each :—
To lie, invulnerable, alone,
Valkyrie and hero, in the zone,
Shielded by lightnings of our wit,
Guarded by fires of intellect
Far on the mountain-top, elect
Of all the hills divinely lit
By rays of moonrise ! O the moon !
O the interminable tune
Of whispered kisses ! Love exults,
Intolerant of all else than he,
And ecstasy invades, insults,
Outshines the waves of harmony,
Lapped in the sun of day ; the tides
Of wonder flow, the shore subsides ;
And over all the horizon
Glows the last glimmer of the sun.
Ah ! when the moon arises, she
Shall look on nothing but the sea.

VII

O LOVE! and were I with thee ever!
Come with me over the round earth,
O'er lake and fountain, sea and river!
Girdle the world with angel girth
Of angel voyage! Shall we roam
In teeming jungles poisonous?
Or make ourselves an eyrie-home
Where the black ice roars ravenous
In glittering avalanche? Or else
Hide in some corrie on the fells
Of heather and bracken, or delight
In grottos built of stalactite?
Or be our lonely haunt the sand
Of the Sahara: let us go
Where some oasis, subtly planned
For love, invites the afterglow!
There let us live alone, except
Some bearded horseman, pennoned, ride
Over the waste of ochre, swept
By wind in waves, and sit beside
Our tent a little, bring us news
Of the great world we have lost for—this!
What fool exclaims—" to lose!"? To lose?
Ah! earth and heaven for one small kiss!
But he shall sing beside our fire
The epic of the world's desire;
How Freedom fares, how Art yet revels
Sane in the dance of dogs and devils.
His thunder voice shall climb and crash,
Scourge liars with tongue's lightning lash,

Through ranks of smitten tyrants drive,
Till bosoms heave, and eyes outflash,
And it is good to be alive.
He shall ride off at dawn, and we
Shall look upon our life again ;
You old, and all your beauty be
Broken, and mine a broken brain.
Yet we shall know ; delighting still
In the sole laughter death derides
In vain ; the indomitable will,
Still burning in the spirit, guides
Our hearts to truth ; we see, we know
How foolish were the things he said,
And answer in the afterglow
How good it is that we are dead.
Will you not come ? Or, where the surf
Beats on the coral, and the palm
Sways slowly in the eternal calm
Of spring, I know a mound of turf
Good for our love to lie on ; good
For breezes, and for sun and shade ;
To hear the murmur of the flood ;
To taste the kava subtly made
To rouse to Bacchic ecstasy,
Since Dionysus silently
Faded from Greece, now only smiles
Amid the soft Hawaiian isles ;
Good, above all the good, to keep
Our bodies when we sleep the sleep.

VIII

MAKE me a roseleaf with your mouth,
And I will waft it through the air
To some far garden of the South,
The herald of our happening there !

Fragrant, caressing, steals the breeze ;
Curls into kisses on your lips :—
I know interminable seas,
Winged ardour of the stately ships,

Space of incalculable blue
And years enwreathed in one close crown,
And glimmering laughters echoing you
From reverend shades of bard's renown :—

Nature alive and glad to hymn
Your beauty, my delight : her God
Weary, his old eyes sad and dim
In his intolerable abode.

All things that are, unknown and known,
Bending in homage to your eyes ;
We wander wondering, lift alone
The world's grey load of agonies.

Make me a roseleaf with your mouth,
That all the savour steal afar
Unto the sad awaiting South,
Where sits enthroned the answering Star.

IX

WILL you not come : the unequal fever
Of Paris hold our lives for ever ?
Were it not better to exceed
The avenging thought, the unmeaning deed,
Make one strong act at least ? How small,
How idiot our lives ! These folk
That think they live—which dares at all
To act ? The suicide that broke
His chain, and lies so waxen pale
In the Morgue to-day ? Did he then fail ?
Ay, he was beaten. But to live,
Slink on through what the world can give,
That is a hound's life too. For me,
The suicide stands grand and free
Beside these others. Was it fear
Drove him to stand upon the bank ?
The Paris lights shone far and drear ;
The mist was down ; the night was dank ;
The Seine ran easily underneath ;
The air was chill : he knew the Seine
By pain would put an end to pain,
And jumped,—and struggled against death,
I doubt not. Ye courageous men
That scorn to flee the world, ye slaves
Of commerce, ye that ply the pen,
That dig, and fill, and loathe your graves !
Ye counter-jumpers, clergy, Jews,
All Paris, smug and good, that use
To point the index scorn, deride
The courage of that suicide—

I ask you not to quit us quite,
But—will you take a bath to-night?
Money might make you. Well : but he,
What was his wage, what was his fee?
Fear fiercer than a mortal fear.
Be silent, cowards, leave him here
Dead in the Morgue, so waxen pale!
He failed : shall ye not also fail?
Ah! love! the strings are little;
    The cords are over strong;
The chain of life is brittle;
    And keen the sword of song.
Will you not seize in one firm grip
Now, as I hold you, lip to lip,
The serpent of Event, hold hard
Its slipping coils, its writhe retard,
And snap its spine? Delicate hands
You have : the work is difficult;
Effort that holds and understands
May do it : shall our foes exult,
The daughters of Philistia laugh,
The girls of Askalon rejoice,
Writing for us this epitaph :
" They chose, and were not worth the choice "?
You are so pure : I am a man.
I will assume the courage tried
Of yonder luckless suicide,
Any you—awaken, if you can,
The courage of the courtezan!

X

TO sea! To sea! The ship is trim;
The breezes bend the sails.
They chant the necromantic hymn,
Arouse Arabian tales.

To sea ! Before us leap the waves ;
The wild white combers follow.
Invoke, ye melancholy slaves,
The morning of Apollo !

There's phosphorescence in the wake,
And starlight o'er the prow.
One comet, like an angry snake,
Lifts up its hooded brow.

The black grows grey toward the East :
A hint of silver glows.
Gods gather to the mystic feast
On interlunar snows.

The moon is up full-orbed : she glides
Striking a snaky ray
Across the black resounding tides,
The sepulchre of day.

The moon is up : upon the prow
We stand and watch the moon.
A star is lustred on your brow ;
Your lips begin a tune,

A long, low tune of love that swells
Little by little, and lights
The overarching miracles
Of love's desire, and Night's.

It swells, it rolls to triumph-song
Through luminous black skies ;
Thrills into silence sharp and strong,
Assumes its peace, and dies.

There is the night : it covers close
The lilies folded fair
of all your beauty, and the rose
Half hidden in your hair.

There is the night : unseen I stand
And look to seaward still :
We would not look upon the land
Again, had I my will.

The ship is trim: to sea! to sea!
Take life in either hand,
Crush out its wine for you and me,
And drink, and understand !

XI

I AM a pretty advocate !
My speech has served me ill. Perchance
Silence had served : you now look straight
On that clear evidence of France,
The embroidered garter yonder. Wait !
I had some confidence in fate
Ere I spoke thus. For while I spoke
The old smile, surely helpless, broke
On your tired lips : the old light woke
In your deep eyes : but silence falls
Blank, blank : the species that appals,
Not our old silence. I devise
A motto for your miseries :
" There an embroidered garter lies,
And here words—they lie too ? " I see
Your intuition of the truth
Is still in its—most charming—youth.
You need that physiology !

XII

I LOVE you. That seems simple ? No !
Hear what the physiologist
Says on the subject. *To and fro*
The motor axis of the brain
Hits on the cerebellum hard,
Makes the medulla itch : the bard
Twitches his spinal cord again,
Excites Rolando's fissure, and
Impinges on the Pineal gland.
Then Hippocampus major strikes
The nerves, and we may say " He likes,"
But if the umbilical cord
Cut the cerebrum like a sword,
And afferent ganglia, sensory bones,
Shake in the caecum : then one groans
" He likes Miss What's your Name." *And if*
The appendix vermiformis biff
The pericardium, pleura shoves
The femur—we may say : " He loves."
Here is the mechanism strange
(But perfectly correct) to change
My normal calm—seraphic dew !
Into an ardent love for you.

XIII

IS there a soul behind the mask ?
What master drives these slaves to task
Thus willing ? Physiology
Wipes the red scalpel, scorns reply.
My argument to please you swerves,
Becomes a mere defence of nerves.
Why they are thus, why so they act,
We know not, but accept the fact.
How this for my peccation serves ?
Marry, how ? Tropically ! Pact
I bind with blood to show you use
For this impertinence—and add
A proverb fit to make you mad
About the gander and the goose,
Till you riposte with all your force
A miserable pun on sauce.
The battle when you will ! This truce
I take in vantage, hold my course.
I see mechanic causes reach
Back through eternity, inform
The stellar drift, the solar storm,
The protoplasmic shiver, each
Little or great, determinate
In law for Fate, the Ultimate.
If this be meaningless, much more
Vacant your speech and sophic skill
(My feminine and fair Escobar !)
To prove mere circumstance is no bar
Against the freedom of the will.
However this may be, we are

Here and not otherwhere, star to star !
Hence then act thou ! Restrain the " Damn ! "
Evoked by " I am that I am."
Perpend ! (Hark back to Hamlet !) If
You stand thus poised upon the cliff
Freewill—I await that will ; (One) laughter ;
(Two) the old kiss ; (Three) silence after.
No ? Then vacate the laboratory !
Psychology must crown the event,
And sociology content,
Ethics suffice, the simple story !
(Oh ! that a woman ever went
Through course of science full and whole,
Without the loss of beauty's scent,
And grace, and subtlety of soul.
Ah God ! this Law maketh hearts ache,
" Who eateth shall not have his cake.")

XIV

ACCEPT me as I am! I give
All you can take. If you dislike
Some fragments of the life I live,
They are not yours : I scorn to strike
One sword-swift pang against your peace.
See ! I'm a mountaineer. Release
That spirit from your bonds : or come
With me upon the mountains, cease
This dull round, this addition sum
Of follies we call France : indeed
Cipher ! And if at times I need
The golden dawn upon the Alps,
The gorges of Himalayan rock,
The grey and ancient hills, the scalps
Of hoary hills, the rattling shock
Of avalanche adown the hills—
Why, what but you, your image, fills
My heart in these ? I want you there.
For whom but you do I ply pen,
Talk with unmentionable men
Of proofs and types—dull things !—for whom
But you am I the lover ? Bloom,
O flower, immortal flower, love, love !
Linger about me and above,
Thou perfumed haze of incense-mist !
The air hath circled me and kissed
Here in this room, on mountains far,
Yonder to seaward, toward yon star,
With your own kisses. Yes ! I see
The roseate embroidery

Yonder—I know : it seems to give
The lie to me in throat and teeth.
That is the surface : underneath
I live in you: in you I live.

XV

WILL you not learn to separate
The essential from the accidental,
Love from desire, caprice from fate,
The inmost from the merely mental?
Our star, the sun, gives life and light:
Let that decay, the aeons drown
Sense in stagnation; death and night
Smite the fallen fragments of the crown
Of spring: but serves the garter so?
What wandering meteor is this
Across the archipelago
Luminous of our starry bliss?
Let that be lost: the smile disputes
The forehead's temple with the frown,
When gravitation's arrow shoots,
And stockings happen to slip down.
You are my heart: the central fire
Whereby my being burns and moves,
The mainspring of my life's desire,
The essential engine that approves
The will to live: and these frail friends,
The women I shall draw you, fail
Of more importance to earth's ends
Than to my life a finger-nail.
'Twere pain, no doubt, were torn away
One, a minute distemperature.
I spend a fraction of the day
Plying the art of manicure.

But always beats the heart : the more
I polish, tint, or carve, I ask
Strength from the heart's too generous store
To bend my fingers to the task.
Cease : I am broken : nought remains.
The brain's electric waves are still ;
No blood beats eager in the veins ;
The mind sinks deathward, and the will.
It is no figure of boy's speech,
Lover's enthusiasm, rhyme
Magniloquent of bard, to reach
Truth through the husk of space and time :
No truth is more devout than this :
" In you I live : I live in you. "
Had Latmos not known Artemis,
Where were the faint lights of that dew
Of Keats ? O maiden moon of mine,
Imperial crescent, rise and shine !

XVI

I WAS a fool to hide it. Here
Phantoms arise and disappear,
Obedient to the master's wand.
The incense curls like a pale frond
Of some grey garden glory about
This room ; I take my sceptre out,
My royal crown ; invoke, evoke
These phantoms in the glimmering smoke ;
And you shall see—and take no hurt—
The very limb yon garter girt.

XVII

I AM a man. Consider first
What we may learn, if but we will,
From that small lecture I rehearsed
With very Huxley's strength and skill
And clarity. What do I mean,
Admitting manhood ? This : to-day
I fed on oysters, ris-de-veau,
Beefsteak and grapes. Will you repay
My meal with anger, rosy grow
With shame because instead of you
I went to feed chez Lavenue ?
The habit anthropophagous,
Nice as it is, is not for us.
I love you : will you share my life,
Become my mistress or my wife ?
Agreed : but can your kisses feed me ?
Is it for dinner that you need me ?
But think : it is for you I eat.
Even as the object that I see,
The brain 'tis pictured in ; the beat
Of nerves that mean the picture are
Not like it, but dissimilar.
How can a nervous current be
Like that Velasquez ? So I find
Dinner a function of the mind,
Not like you, but essential to
(Even it) my honest love of you.
Consider then yon broidered toy
In the same aspect ! Steals no joy
Glittering beneath the sad pale face ?

XVIII

STILL grave, my budding Arahat?
I see the crux of my disgrace
Lies in the mad idea that—that!—
Is not dissimilar, usurps
The very function I have given
Blissful beyond the bliss of heaven—
Aha! there is a bird that chirps
Another song. Here's paint and brush
And canvas. I will paint anon
The limb yon garter once was on;
Sketch you a nude—my soul—and nude
The very human attitude
We all assume—or else are posers.
Such winners are the surest losers.
I paint her picture, recognise—
Dare you? one glimmer of her eyes
Like yours, one shimmer of her skin
Like that your flesh is hidden in,
One laugh upon her lips enough
Like yours for me to recollect,
Remind, recall, hint? Never! Stuff!
You are, as aye, alone, elect.
Shall we then dive in Paris sewers?
Ay! but not find you there, nor yet
Your likeness. Did you then forget
You are my love? Arise and shine!
It was your blasphemy, not mine.

XIX

A FAINT sweet smell of ether haunts
Yet the remembrance. Hear the wizard
His lone and melancholy chaunts
Roared in the rain-storm and the blizzard !
The ancient and devoted dizzard !
Appear, thou dream of loveliness !
She wore a rose and amber dress,
With broidery of old gold. Her hair
Was long and starry, gilded red.
Her face was laughter, shapen fair
By the sweet things she thought and said.
Her whiteness rustled as she walked.
Her hair sang tunes across the air.
She sighed, laughed, whispered, never talked.
She smiled, and loves devout and rare
Flickered about the room. She stayed
Still in the dusk : her body sang
Out full and clear " O love me ! " Rang
The silver couplets undismayed,
Bright, bold, convincing. In her eyes
Glittered enamelled sorceries.
She was a piece of jewel work
Sold by a Christian to a Turk.
She had fed on air that day : the flowers
About her curled, ambrosial bowers
Of some divine perfume : the soul
Of ether made her wise ; control
Of strong distilled delight. She showered
Wit and soft laughter and desire
About her breasts in bliss embowered,

And subtle and devouring fire
Leapt in live sparks about her limbs.
Her spirit shields me, and bedims
My sight : she needs me : I need her.
She is mine : she calls me : sob and stir
Strange pulses of old passionate
Imperial ecstasies of fate.
Destiny ; manhood ; fear ; delight ;
Desire ; accomplishment ; ere night
Dipped her pail plumes to greet the sun
She was not ; all is past and done.
A dream ? I wake from blissful sleep,
But is it real ? Well, I keep
An accidental souvenir
Whence thus to chronicle small beer ;
There is the garter. Launched our boat,
The stately pinnace once afloat,
You shall hear all ; we will not land
On this or that mediate strand,
Until the voyage be done, and we
Pass from the river to the sea,
And find some isle's secluded nook
More sacred than we first forsook.

XX

YES, there are other phases, dear !
Here is a pocket-book, and here
Lies a wee letter. Floral thyrse ?
Divine-tipped narthex of the pine,
Or morphia's deceitful wine ?
The French is ill, the spelling worse !—
But this is horrible ! This, me ?
The upholder of propriety,
Who actually proposed to form
A club to shield us from the swarm
Of common people of no class
Who throng the Quartier Montparnasse !
I wear a collar : loudly shout
That folk are pigs that go without,—
And here you find me up a tree
To make my concierge blush for me !
A girl " uncombed, so badly dressed,
So rudely mannered—and the rest ;
Not at all proper. Fie ! away !
What would your lady mother say ? "
I tell you, I was put to it
To wake a wonder of my wit
Winged, to avail me from the scorn
Of my own concierge. Adorn
The facts I might ; you know them not ;
But that were just the one black blot
On this love's lesson : still, to excuse
Myself to you, who could not choose

But make some weak apology
Before the concierge's eye !
True, you are far too high to accuse—
Perhaps would rather not be told ?
You shall hear. Does a miner lose
If through the quartz he gets to gold ?
Yes : Nina was a thing of nought,
A little laughing lewd gamine,
Idle and vicious, void of thought,
Easy, impertinent, unclean—
Utterly charming ! Yes, my queen !
She had a generous baby soul,
Prattled of love. Should I control,
Repress perhaps the best instinct
The child had ever had ? I winked
At foolish neighbours, did not shirk.
Such café Turc I made her drink
As she had never had before ;
Set her where you are sitting ; chatted ;
Found where the fires of laughter lurk ;
Played with her hair, tangled and matted ;
Fell over strict nice conduct's brink,
Gave all she would, and something more.
She was an honest little thing,
Gave of her best, asked no response.
What more could Heaven's immortal king
Censed with innumerous orisons ?
So, by that grace, I recognised
A something somewhere to be prized
Somewhat. What portress studies song ?
My worthy concierge was wrong.

XXI

THEN let not memory shrink abashed,
Once started on this giddy whirl!
Hath not a lightning image flashed
Of my divine boot-button girl?
She is a dainty acrobat,
Tailor-made from tip to toe;
A tiniest coquettish hat,
A laughing face alight, aglow
With all the fun of life. She comes
Often at morning, laughs aloud
At the poor femm de ménage; hums
Some dancing tune, invades my cloud
Of idle dreams, sits poised upon
The couch, and with a gay embrace
Cries out " Hullo, my baby!" Shone
Such nature in a holier face?
We are a happy pair at least:
Coffee and rolls are worth a feast,
And laughing as she came she goes!
The dainty little tuberose!
She has a lithe white body, slim
And limber, fairy-like, a snake
Hissing some Babylonian hymn
Tangled in the Assyrian brake.
She stole upon me as I slept:
Who wonders I am nympholept?
Her face is round and hard and small
And pretty—hence the name I gave her
Of the boot-button girl. Appal
These words? Ah, would your spirit save her?

She's right just as she is : so wise
You look through hardly-opened eyes
One would believe you could do better.
Ma foi ! And is your God your debtor ?
So, my true love, I paint you three
Portraits of women that love me.

XXII

THESE portraits, darling, are they yours?
And yet there sticks the vital fact
That these, as you, are women. Lures
The devil of the inexact
With subtle leasing? Nay! O nay!
I'll catch him with a cord, draw out
By a bent fish-hook through his snout,
Give to my maiden for a play.
You, they, and dinner and—what else?—
However unlike, coincide
In composition verified
Of final protoplasmic cells.
Shall this avail to stagger thought,
Confuse the reason, bring to nought
The rosebud, in reflecting: Hem!
What beauty hath the flower and stem?
Carbon we know, and nitrogen,
And oxygen—are these a rose?
But this though everybody knows,
That this should be the same for men
They know not. Death may decompose,
Reduce to primal hyle perchance—
I shall not do it in advance!
So let the accidental fact
That these are women, fall away
To black oblivion: be the pact
Concluded firm enough to-day,
Not thus to err. So you are not

In essence or in function one
With these, the unpardonable blot
On knighthood's shield, the sombre spot
Seen on the photosphere of sun.

XXIII

" NAY ! that were nothing," say you now,
Poor baby of the weary brow,
Struggling with metaphysic lore ?
" But these, being women, gave you more :
" You spoke of love ! " Indeed I did,
And you must counter me unbid,
Forgetting how we must define
This floral love of yours and mine.
That love and this are as diverse
As Shelley's poems and my verse.
And now the bright laugh comes in spite
Of all the cruel will can do.
" I take," you say, " a keen delight
In Shelley, but as much in you."
There, you are foolish. And you know
The thing I meant to say. O love !
What little lightnings serve to show
Glimpses of all your heart ! Above
All, and beneath all, lies there deep,
Canopied over with young sleep,
Bowered in the lake of nenuphars,
Watched by the countless store of stars,
The abiding love you bear me. Hear
How perfect love casts flying fear
Forth from its chambers ! Those and this
Are utterly apart. The bliss
Of this small quarrel far exceeds
That dervish rapture, dancer deeds
Strained for egregious emphasis.
These touch you not ! You sit alone

Passionless upon passion's throne,
And there is love. Look not below,
Lest aught disturb the silver flow
Of harmonies of love ! Awake !
Awake for love's own solar sake !
Diverse devotion we divide
From the one overflowing tide.
Despise this fact ! So lone and far
Lies the poor garter, that I gaze
Thither ; it casts no vivid rays.
But hither ? I behold the star !

XXIV

NOW your grave eyes are filled with tears ;
Your hands are trembling in my own ;
The slow voice falls upon my ears,
An undulating monotone.
Your lips are gathered up to mine :
Your bosom heaves with fearful breath ;
Your scent is keen as floral wine,
Inviting me, and love, to death.
You, whom I kept, a sacred shrine,
Will fling the portals to the day ;
Where shone the moon the sun shall shine,
Silver in scarlet melt away.
There is a yet a pang : they give me this
Who can ; and you who could have failed ?
Is it too late to extend the kiss ?
Too late the goddess be unveiled ?
O but the generous flower that gives
Her kisses to violent sun,
Yet none the less in ardour lives
An hour, and then her day is done.
Back from my lips, back from my breast !
I hold you as I always will,
You unprofaned and uncaressed,
Silent, majestical, and still.
Back ! for I love you. Even yet
Do you not see my deepest fire
Burn through the veils and coverings set
By fatuous phantoms of desire ?
Back ! O I love you evermore.
But, be our bed the bridal sky !

I love you, love you. Hither, shore
Of far unstained eternity !
There we will rest. Beware ! Beware !
For I am young, and you are fair.
Nay! I am old in this, you know !
Ah ! heat of God ! I love you so !

XXV

O WHAT pale thoughts like gum exude
From smitten stem of tropic tree !
I talk of veils, who love the nude !
Witness the masterpieces three
Of Rodin that make possible
Life in prosaic Paris, stand
About the room, its chorus swell
From the irritating to the grand.
Shall we, who love the naked form,
The inmost truth, to ourselves fail,
Take shelter from love's lightning-storm
Behind some humbug's hoary veil ?
Ah ! were it so, love, could the flame
Of fast electric fervour flash,
Smite us through husk of form and name,
Leave of the dross a little ash,
One button of pure fuséd gold
Identical—O floral hour !
That were the bliss no eyes behold,
But Christ's delighted bridal dower
Assuming into God the Church.
But—oh ! these nudes of Rodin ! I
Drag one more linnet from its perch
That sang to us, and sang a lie.
Did Rodin strip the clothes, and find
A naked truth fast underneath ?
Never ! Where lurks the soul and mind ?
What is the body but a sheath ?
Did he ply forceps, scalpel, saw,
Tear all the grace of form apart,

Intent to catch some final law
Behind the engine of the heart ?
He tried not ; whoso has, has failed.
So, did I pry beneath the robe,
Till stubborn will availed, nor quailed,
Intimate with naked probe ?
I know the husks to strip ; name, form,
Sensation, then perception, stress
Of nature thither ; last, the swarm
Of honey-bees called consciousness.
These change and shape a myriad shapes.
Diverse are these, not one at all,
What gain I if my scalpel scrapes,
Turning before some final wall
Of soul ? Not so, nothing is there.
The qualities are all : for this
I stop as I have stopped ; intrude
No science, for I love the fair ;
No wedlock, for I love the kiss ;
No scalpel, for I love the nude.
And we await the deep event.
Whate'er it be, in solitude ;
Silent, with ecstasy bedewed ;
Content, as Rodin is content.

XXVI

I WILL not, and you will not. Stay !
Do you recall that night of June
When from the insufferable day
Edged out the dead volcanic moon
Solemn into midnight ? You
Shown your inviolate violet eyes
Into my eyes less sad, and drew
Back from the slender witcheries
Of word and song : and silence knew
What splendour in the silence lies,
The soul drawn back into itself.
It was the deep environing
Wood that then shielded us : the elf
And fairy in an emerald ring,
And hamadryad of the trees,
And naiad of the sleepy lake,
That watched us on the mossy leas
Look on each other's face, and take
The secret of the universe
to sleep with us : you knew, and I,
The purport of the eternal curse,
The ill design of destiny.
You know, and I, O living head
Of love ! the things that were not said.

XXVII

DO you recall ? Could I forget ?
How once the full moon shone above,
Over the houses, and we let
Loose rein upon the steeds of love ?
How kisses fled to kisses, rain
Of fiery dew upon the soul
Kindled, till ecstasy was pain ;
Desire, delight : and swift control
Leapt from the lightning, as the cloud
Disparted, rended, from us twain,
And we were one : the aerial shroud
Closed on us, shall not lift again
For aught we do : O glamour grown
Inseparable and alone !
And then we knew as now the tune
Our lives were set to, and sang back
Across the sky toward the moon
Into the cloud's dissolving wrack,
Vanished for ever. And we found
Coprolite less than chrysolite,
Flowers fairer than their food, the ground ;
We knew our destiny, saw how
Man's fate is written on his brow,
And how our love throughout was hewn
And masked and moulded by the moon.

XXVIII

AND who is then the moon ? Bend close,
And clothe me in a silken kiss,
And I will whisper to my rose
The secret name of Artemis.
Words were not needed then : to-day
Must I begin what never I thought
To do : mould flowers in common clay ?
Mud casket of mere words is nought,
When by love's miracle we guess
What either always thinketh. Yes ?

XXIX

SO, love, not thus for you and me!
And if I am man, no more, expect
I shall remain so, till, maybe,
The anatomist, old Time, dissect
Me, nerve from flesh, and bone from bone,
And raise me spiritual, changed
In all but love for you, my own;
The little matter rearranged,
The little mind refigured. This
Alone I hope or think to keep :—
The love I bear you, and the kiss
Too soft to call the breath of sleep.
And, if you are woman, even there
I do decline : we stand above.
I ask not, and will take no share
With you in what mankind call love.
We know each other : you and I
Have nought to do with lesser things.
With them—'tis chance or destiny :
With us, we should but burn our wings.
We love, and keep ourselves apart :
Mouth unto mouth, heart unto heart,
Thus ever, never otherwise.
The soul is out of me, and swings
In desperate and strange surmise
About the inmost heart of things.
This is all strange : but is not life,
Death, all, most strange, not to be told,
Not to be understood by strife
Of brain, nor bought for gleaming gold,

Nor known by aught but love? And love
Far from resolving soul to sense,
Stands isolated and above
Immaculate, alone, intense,
Concentrate on itself. But should
The lesser leave me, as it might;
The lesser never touch you; would
Your will be one with my delight?
Leave all the thoughts and miseries!
Invade the glowing fields of sun!
Cross bleak inhospitable seas,
Until this hour be past and done,
And we in some congenial clime
Are then reborn, where danger's nought
To mock the old Parisian time
When fear was still the child of thought!
So we could love, and love, and fate
Never clang brutal on the gong,
And lunch, man-eating tiger, wait
Crouched in the jungles of my song;
My gaze be steadfast on the star
And never to the garter glide,
And I on rapture's nenuphar
Sit Buddha-like above the tide.

XXX

O BLUEBELL of the inmost wood,
Before whose beauty I abase
My head, and bind my burning blood,
And hide within the moss my face,
I would not so—or not for that
Would so : the gods knew well to save
The mountain summit from the flat,
Youth's laughter from its earlier grave.
It is a better love, exists
Only because of these below it :
Mountains loom grander in the mists :
The lover's foolish to the poet.
I know. Far better strive and earn
The rest you give me than remain
Ever upon the heights that burn
Sunward, and quite forget the plain.
Beauteous and bodiless we are ;
Rapture is our inheritance ;
You shine, an everlasting star,
I, the rough nebula : but whence,
Whither, we know not. But we know
That if our joy were always so
We might not know it. Strange indeed
This earth where all is paradox,
Pushed to the truth : what lies succeed
When every truth essential mocks
Its truth in figure of a phrase ?
How should I care for this, and tire
Body by will to sing thy praise,
Who take this lute, throw down the lyre

As I have done to-day, to win
No guerdon differing from the toil,
Were that accomplished : pain and sin
Are needed for the counterfoil
Of joy and love ; if only so
All men had these in keen excess
Those were forgotten : indigo
Is amber's shadow, but—confess
For all men but ourselves the tint
Of all the earth is dull and black !
Only some glints of love bestow
The knowledge of what meteor wrack
Trails pestilence across the sky.
But we are other—you and I !
So shall we live in deep content,
Unchanging bliss, despise them still
Groping on isle and continent
Wreathed in the mesh of woe and ill ?
Ah! Zeus! we will not: be the law
Of uttermost compassion ours !
Our snows it shall not come to thaw,
Nor burn the roses from our bowers.

XXXI

AY ! There's a law ! For this recede,
Hide with me in the deepest caves
Of some volcanic island ; bleed
Our hearts out by the ambient waves
Of Coromandel ; live alone,
Hermits of love and pity, far
Where tumbled banks of ice are thrown,
Watched by yon solitary star,
Sirius ; there to work together
In sorrow and in joy but one,
In black inhospitable weather,
Or fronting the Numidian sun,
Equally minded ; till the hour
Strike of release, and we obtain
The passionless and holy power,
Making us masters over pain,
And lords of peace : the rays of light
We fling to the awakening globe ;
The cavern of the eremite
Shall glow with inmost fire, a robe
Of diamond energy, shall flash
Even to the confines of wide space ;
Comets their tails in fury lash
To look on our irradiate face.
And we will heal them. Dragon men
And serpent women, worm and clod,
Shall rise and look upon us then,
And know us to be very God,
Finding a saviour in the sight

Of power attaining unto peace,
And meditation's virgin might
Pregnant with twins—love and release.
Are you not ready ? Let us leave
This little Paris to its fate !
Our friends a little while may grieve,
And then forget : but we, elate,
Live in a larger air : awake,
Compassion in the Halls of Truth !
Disdain love for love's very sake !
Take all our beauty, strength, and youth,
And melt them in the crucible
To that quintessence at whose gleam
Gold shudders and grows dull ; expel
The final dross by intimate steam
Of glowing truth, our lunar light !
Are you not ready ? Who would stay ?
Arise, O Queen, O Queen of Night !
Arise, and leave the little day !

XXXII

LADY, awake the dread abyss
Of knowledge in impassioned eyes !
Fathom the gulphs of awful bliss
With the poised plummet of a kiss !

Love hath the arcanum of the wise ;
Love is the elixir, love the stone ;
The rosy tincture shall arise
Out of its shadowy cadences.

Love is the Work, and love alone
Rewards the ingenious alchemist.
Chaste fervours chastely overthrown
Awake the infinite monotone.

So, Lady, if thy lips I kissed ;
So, lady, if in eyes of steel
I read the steady secret, wist
Of no gray ghosts moulded of mist ;

I did not bid my purpose kneel,
Nor thine retire : I probe the scar
Of self, the goddess keen and real
Supreme within the naked wheel

Of sun and moon and star and star,
And find her but the ambient coil,
Imagination's avatar,
A Buddha on his nenuphar

Elaborate of Indian toil;
A mockery of a self; outrun
Its days and dreams, its strength and spoil,
As runs the conquering counterfoil.

Thou art not; thou the moon and sun,
Thou the sole star in trackless night,
The unguessed spaces one by one
That mask their Sphinx, the horizon:

Thou, these; and one above them, light,
Light of the inmost heaven and hell :—
Art changed and fallen and lost to sight,
Who wast as waters of delight.

And I, who am not, know thee well
Who art not: then the chain divides
From love-enlightened limbs, and swell
The choral cries unutterable.

Out of the salt, out of the tides,
The sea, whose drink is death by thirst!
The triumph anthem overrides
The ocean's lamentable sides,

And we are done with life; accurst
Who linger; lost who find; but we
Follow the gold wake of the first
Who found in losing; who reversed

The dictates of eternity.
Lo! in steep meditation hearsed,

Coffined in knowledge, fast we flee
Unto the island from the sea.

XXXIII

THE note of the silence is changed ; the quarrel is over
That rather endeared than estranged : lover to lover
Flows in the infinite river of knowledge and peace :
Not a ripple or eddy or quiver : the monitors cease
That were eager to warn, to awaken : a sleep is opposed,
And the leaves of the rose wind-shaken are curled and closed ;
Gone down in the glare of the sun ; and the twilight perfumes
Steal soft in the wake of the One that abides in the glooms.
Walking he is, and slowly ; thoughtful he seems,
Pure and happy and holy ; as one would who dreams
In the day-time of deep delights no kin to the day,
But a flower new-born of the night's in Hecate's way.
Love is his name, and he bears the ill quiver no more.
He has aged as we all, and despairs ; but the lady who bore
Him, Eros, to ruin the ages, has softened at heart ;
He is tamed by the art of the sages, the magical art.
No longer he burns and blisters, consumes and corrodes ;
He hath Muses nine for sisters ; the holy abodes
Of the maiden are open to him, for his wrath is grown still ;
His eyes with weeping are dim ; he hath changed his will.
We know him ; and Venus sinks, a star in the West ;
A star in the even, that thinks it shall fall into rest.
Let it be so, then ! Arise, O moon of the lyrical spears !
Huntress, O Artemis wise, be upon him who hears !
I have heard thy clear voice in the moon ; I have borne it afar ;
I have tuned it to many a tune ; thou hast showed me a star,
And the star thou hast showed me I follow through uttermost
    night.
I have shaken my spear at Apollo ; his ruinous might
I have mocked, I have mastered. All hail to the Star of

   Delight
That is tender and fervid and frail, and avails me aright !
Hail to thee, symbol of love, assurance and promise of peace !
Stand fast in the skies above, till the skies are abolished and
   cease !
And for me, may I never forget how things came well as they
   are !
It was long I had wandered yet ere my eyes found out the star.
Be silent, love, and abide ; the wanton strings must go
To the vain tumultuous tide of the spirit's overflow.
I sing and sing to the world ; then silence soon
Be about us clasped and furled in the light of the moon.
Forget not, never forget the terrible song I have sung ;
How the eager fingers fret the lute, and loose the tongue
Tinkles delicate things, faint thoughts of a futile past—
We are past on eagle wings, and the silence is here at last.
The last low wail of the lyre, be it soft with a tear
For the children of earth and fire that have brought us here.
Give praise, O masterful maid, to Nina, and all as they die !
The moon makes blackest of shade ; the star's in the swarthiest
   sky.
Be silent, O radiant martyr ! Let the world fade slowly afar !
But—had it not been for the Garter, I might never have seen
   the Star.

ΟΥΝ ΑΓΝΟΩΝ ΕΥΣΕΒΕΙΣ

ΕΓΩ ΡΟΔΟΣ ΚΑΤΑΓΓΕΛΛΩ ΣΟΙ

www.ingramcontent.com/pod-product-compliance
Lightning Source LLC
LaVergne TN
LVHW041459070426
835507LV00009B/682